A Williamson *Quick Starts for Kids!*® Book

Make Your Own
Puppets
& Puppet Theaters

Carolyn Carreiro

Illustrated by Norma Jean Martin-Jourdenais

Williamson Books • Nashville, Tennessee

Library of Congress Cataloging-in-Publication Data

Carreiro, Carolyn, 1961-
    Make your own puppets & puppet theaters / Carolyn Carreiro ;
illustrated by Norma Jean Martin-Jourdenais.
      p. cm. -- (A Williamson quick starts for kids! book)
    Includes index.
    ISBN 0-8249-6770-4 (pbk. : alk. paper) -- ISBN 0-8249-6776-3
(hardcover : alk. paper)
    1. Puppet making--Juvenile literature. 2. Puppet theaters--Design
and construction--Juvenile literature.   I. Martin-Jourdenais, Norma Jean.
II. Title. III. Series.
TT174.7.C37 2005
745.592'24--dc22

2005014256

Quick Starts for Kids!® series editor: Susan Williamson
Project editor: Michelle Peters
Interior illustrations: Norma Jean Martin-Jourdenais
Interior design: Linda Williamson/Dawson Design
Cover illustrations: Mike Kline
Cover design: Marie Ferrante-Doyle
Printed and bound in Italy by LEGO

Williamson Books
An imprint of Ideals Publications
A division of Guideposts
535 Metroplex Drive, Suite 250
Nashville, Tennessee 37211
www.idealsbooks.com
(800) 586-2572

10 9 8 7 6 5 4 3 2 1

Books by Carolyn Carreiro

HAND-PRINT ANIMAL ART
(a Williamson *Kids Can!*® Book)

For my children, Laura and Sam,
for my nieces and nephews,
Emma, Daniel, Maisie, and Theo,
and for all the other children in
my life, Neil, Jean Philippe, and
Nicolas, Joseph, Annie, Julia,
and Molly, Lily, and Eliza.

ACKNOWLEDGMENTS
Thank you, Neil, for napping
while I made puppets. Thank
you, Laura, for helping, and
Sam for only playing your
drums while I was out.
Everything in life is easier and
more fun when you're happy.
Thank you, Philippe, for making
me happy.

CONTENTS

Puppets! Puppets! Puppets!

11 QUICK STARTS PUPPET & PUPPETEER QUESTIONS WITH ANSWERS!

I'm 12 and I'm not sure I should play with puppets. Are puppets just for little kids?

Maybe you're confusing puppets and puppet shows. Older kids and adults make most puppets. And professional puppeteers, like the people who are working on Sesame Street, are definitely adults. Puppet shows can be for people of all different ages. Of course, you may know all about Kermit the Frog, Miss Piggy, Bert, Ernie, and the gang. And you probably watched Mr. Rogers with all of his puppets, too. There was a recent puppet show on Broadway in New York called Avenue Q that was for adults. There used to be a show on television called Kukla, Fran, and Ollie that kids and their parents loved. And guess what? Ollie was a one-toothed dragon and Fran was a real person. So, to get back to your question, every age is a great age for puppets!

How do you get started with all of this puppet stuff?

Well, you're at the right place for a very quick start! It's no big deal to start, and then the only real limit is your imagination. That's what is so much fun about puppets — you can make them to be anything you want, from an animal to a talking teapot. And you can make them out of just about anything!

I'm really shy and the librarian at our school told me that she was shy, too. She did a lot of read-alouds with puppets to help her get "out of her shell." But, I don't know if I could do that!

You have a very smart librarian. Puppets are a great way to overcome shyness because you can have the puppet say what is on your mind. Or, you can try on different characters by reading books aloud with your friends, each of you reading different characters. It's a lot of fun and you'll forget all about being shy.

If I make puppets, do I have to be in puppet shows?

No way! There aren't any "have to's" with puppets. This is about fun. You can express yourself either by making puppets or by being a puppeteer. Or, if you like, you can do both. That's the idea behind puppets — it's total freedom to use your imagination in whichever way works best for you.

I know little kids like puppets, but are there any that are safe for them? I'd like to make some and play with them when I am babysitting. What are the easiest ones?

You sound like a great babysitter. Puppets are fun to make and they are a good way to distract kids if they are upset about something. You can cheer up someone who is sad because his mom and dad just went out, and you can use them for someone who is sick or is in the hospital.

Small children love finger puppets. You can make simple finger puppets with felt, construction paper, and brown-paper coin tubes decorated with markers. You could make the child's favorite character from a book and read the story using the puppet as a prop. In this book, you'll find envelope puppets that are sure to be a hit with young children.

Remember, when playing with puppets with young children, take care that the craft supplies you use cannot cause choking. Any object that can pass through a toilet tissue tube is too small for a child under 3 years old to play with. Decorate with markers instead of buttons or beads.

I have chosen to do a puppet show as part of a school book report, but I am not sure where to start. Any ideas?

Without even realizing it, you have already started. You have read a book, so you have a story line on which to base your puppet show. If the book is long, choose a chapter or a scene and the characters from that part of the book. Decide who is the main character, what the story is about, and where the story takes place. You need a beginning, a middle, and an end — hopefully a happy ending — where something wrong has been resolved. You may choose to narrate your puppet show.

Give a little information about the book and the parts of the story leading up to and following the part you choose to tell with puppets. Most of all, have fun!

Do I need to buy an elaborate theater for my puppet show?

No need to raid the piggy bank yet, as theaters of all kinds are easy and inexpensive to make. Depending on the size of your puppets, your theater can be as small as a tissue box or as large as a refrigerator box. See pages 47–48 for some ideas to get you started.

Where can I learn more about puppets?

With an adult's permission, visit the many online sites that can be found using the keywords "Puppetry Exhibits and Museums." There are puppet festivals held all over the world and there are museums and exhibitions where you can go to see famous and historical puppets and learn about the origins of puppetry.

I have so many old stuffed animals. Is there any way I can transform them into puppets?

Making an old stuffed animal come alive is simple, but ask permission first, because it may be someone's favorite. Depending on the size and type of stuffed animal you want to use, either place your entire hand into the back of the body of the stuffed animal or your thumb, pointer, and middle finger into the back of the head. You may need to remove a little stuffing from the head where you insert your fingers or from the body where you place your hand. Use your fingers to move the face while it "talks."

If I don't have an audience for rehearsals, how can I tell if everything looks good from in front of my puppet theater?

There are several things that you can do: Ask someone if he can watch while you do a quick "run-through," which means that you go through the show quickly, skipping long speeches, just to see how everything works on stage. Or, you could have a dress rehearsal with some guests in the audience, and ask them what they think afterward. Or, place a large mirror where your audience will be sitting and watch from behind your puppets, or set up a video camera and tape the show to watch and critique later. Remember that once the audience is seated there will be background noise, so allow for this when deciding how loud to speak.

Are these puppets difficult to make?

The great thing about these puppets is that anyone can make any of them. Look for the "Smiling Fish" symbol next to each puppet. The symbols stand for the amount of effort that goes into making the puppet — the more symbols you see, the more involved the project is.

Getting Started

WHY MAKE PUPPETS?

Puppet-making can be as involved or as simple as you would like it to be; some puppets take minutes to make, and others could take hours. You don't have to be an artist, a sculptor, or a tailor to be a puppet-maker or puppeteer (the person who uses puppets in a show). You don't need to be a musician, an electrician, or a carpenter to create shows and puppet theaters.

Through the puppets you make and use, you can become whoever you'd like to become. It's in your hands — literally! You'll discover the creativity and imagination you never knew you had while making puppets. Every kid and adult is a puppeteer and puppet-maker — just let the characters of your imagination come to life. Try on a new voice, or a different personality; have fun being super silly or serious, or something totally alien!

Remember that without you, puppets are just a pile of cloth, dowels, and cardboard waiting to spring to life. So express yourself through puppets, make your stories come alive, and add animation and fun to your living room or classroom.

PUPPETS CAN BE AS SIMPLE OR AS DETAILED AS YOU WANT!

There's a puppet for every level of interest. You can make super-simple (yet incredibly innovative) puppets out of your painted hands, paper envelopes, and old socks or gloves — no fancy craft materials needed. Use what you have around the house.

Let your creative mind and imagination build on these ideas to create your own people, characters, and creatures. If you can make a hedgehog, you can make a mouse; if you can make an octopus, you can make an imaginary undersea monster. You can have famous guests appearing in your puppet show — how about Spiderman, The Cat in the Hat, or Harry Potter? Bring characters from history books back to life. What better (or more fun) way to learn about George Washington and Martin Luther King Jr.?

TAKE CONTROL OF YOUR SHOW.

The recipe for a successful puppet show begins with imagination and creativity, a splash of music, a beam or two of light, a handful of props, and a mind full of entertaining story ideas.

By making puppets yourself, you get to decide all the details of your character, down to the shoes it wears, the expression on its face, its wild hair (or mane!), how it behaves, and what it says.

For very little money, you can create a puppet through which to express your feelings and ideas. Is there a subject that you would like others to think about? Do you want to show how words can cause hurt feelings? Do you have a particular experience or interest that you want to share with your peers? Make a few puppets, think of how you want to express your ideas, thoughts, and concerns — and let the show begin!

If you want to create a puppet show with more details, then you can add to the experience by writing a script, painting scenery, making theaters and props, and experimenting with sound and lighting effects. You'll be amazed at how this type of professional puppet production gets your message across. You may also be amazed at what fun you will have!

If you're filled with ideas and can't wait to get started, then go ahead and follow your imagination. Use this book to find some new techniques. If you're a little hesitant, my advice is to jump in, get started, and don't think too much about what you're making. Let your hands do the talking, so to speak. Most of all, let go and enjoy the fun of puppets!

A FEW SAFETY TIPS

Make sure you use adequate ventilation if working indoors, work where young children cannot reach scraps or equipment, and be extra cautious and ask for permission and/or help when using anything hot or sharp.

CUTTING CARDBOARD AND PLASTIC JUGS: For some puppets and puppet theaters, you will need to use cardboard boxes or plastic jugs. Ask an adult to cut through the cardboard with an X-Acto knife. These knives are very sharp and for adult use only. Always cover the work surface.

CHILD-SAFETY SCISSORS: Remember to use child-safety scissors when younger children are participating in any craft, or if there is a big group working in a small space. The newer ones cut well.

HOT GLUE GUN: For some of the puppets and puppet theaters, a hot glue gun is suggested. The glue can burn you if it is not cooled properly and the nozzle of the gun can get extremely hot. Always ask for permission to use and for adult supervision when using a hot glue gun.

SMALL OBJECTS: If there are young children around, especially those ages 5 and under, keep small objects out of reach, off the floor, and away from the edges of the table. This includes pieces of popped balloon and aluminum foil, beads, buttons, sequins, wiggly eyes, and small lids and containers. Toddlers are easily tempted to grab these and put them in their mouths, causing a very serious choking hazard.

Fast & Fun
Paper Puppets

Poster board, envelopes, milk and egg cartons — these around-the-house or around-the-classroom materials are the main ingredients for FAST & FUN PAPER PUPPETS. Bring them to life with a little glue, some paint, and a few craft supplies. These inexpensive puppets are simple to make in a flash and great rainy day projects, too!

Milk Carton Bird of Paradise

It's time to raid the recycle bin! There are plenty of useful puppet materials to be found. For this colorful bird of paradise, look for an empty milk carton.

To MAKE THE MILK CARTON BIRD of PARADISE

1 Using a ruler and a pencil, draw a straight line around the center of the carton.

2 Cut out around three sides of the carton, leaving one side uncut.

3 Open the carton and fold as shown. Wipe the inside with a paper towel, if it is still wet.

4 Paint your bird of paradise — and be colorful! Once the paint is dry, use buttons, felt, fabric, glitter, paint, pom poms, colored glues, tissue paper, construction paper, and whatever else you can find to make your puppet beautiful, funny, or elegant.

MATERIALS

Ruler
Pencil
1 milk carton, 1/2 gallon (1.89 liters), well washed and rinsed
Scissors
Paper towel
Tempera paints, any colors, mixed with a little dish detergent
Paintbrushes
Small lids or containers for paint
White glue
Assorted supplies for decoration

Quick Starts Tips!™
Keeping Colors Bright
Remember to keep your paints separate from each other, in different lids and containers. Use separate paintbrushes, too. This way, the colors won't turn muddy.

Egg Carton Monster

Do you need a fierce dragon in your puppet kingdom? Or a sneaky alligator in your jungle? Sure to give your audience a scare, the EGG CARTON MONSTER will do the trick, and it's quick and easy to make!

MATERIALS

1/2 cardboard egg carton, {6 egg cups}
Pencil
3 elastic bands
Scissors
Tempera paints, any colors
Paintbrushes
Small lids or containers for paint
White poster board, scraps
White glue
Black marker
Orange tissue paper, scraps
Long colorful sock

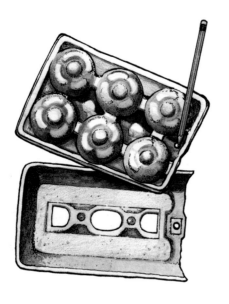

TO MAKE THE EGG CARTON MONSTER

1 Place the egg carton so that the egg cups are on the top. Use the pencil to poke one small hole in both the top and bottom sections.

2 Cut one elastic band and thread it through the holes. Tie the band loosely, so that the jaw can move easily.

EGG CARTON MONSTER

3 Poke two holes side by side on the top and also on the bottom as shown.

4 Cut two elastic bands and thread each through one set of holes. To make the finger grips, tie each band so it makes a loop.

5 Paint your monster. Let dry.

6 Cut out two strips of teeth from the poster board and glue them to the upper and lower jaws just inside the mouth.

7 Cut out two circles from poster board for eyes, draw in the pupils with the black marker, and glue them to the puppet.

8 Cut out flame shapes from the orange tissue paper and glue them just inside the mouth. If you like, wear a long colorful sock on your hand and arm while operating this puppet.

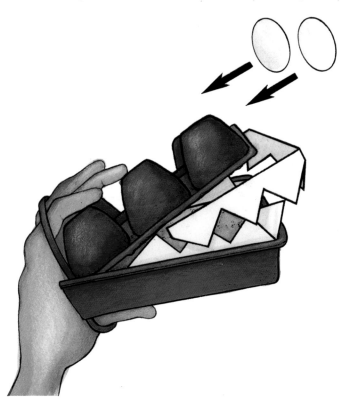

More Quick Starts® Fun!

Using this same idea, you can make an alligator. Paint him green and leave out the flames.

QUICK STARTS EXTRAS!
Owl Finger Puppet

Cut out a bird shape from poster board, make two holes for your thumb and pointer finger, and decorate! You could also make a ballerina, using your fingers as legs.

FOUR ENVELOPE PUPPETS

Your envelope puppets all begin in the same way — plain, flat, rectangular envelopes. Then, with a few folds, a little paint, some glue, and craft supplies, they're not just envelopes anymore! Just slide your hand inside and push in a little between your thumb and pointer finger to create the mouth.

1 Paper-Chain Wriggly Snake

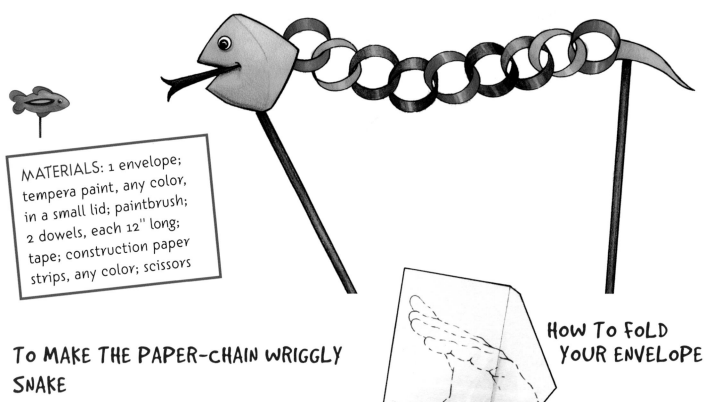

MATERIALS: 1 envelope; tempera paint, any color, in a small lid; paintbrush; 2 dowels, each 12" long; tape; construction paper strips, any color; scissors

TO MAKE THE PAPER-CHAIN WRIGGLY SNAKE

1 Fold envelope as shown. Paint the envelope snake head, let dry, and tape it to a dowel.

2 Make a colorful paper chain with the construction paper strips and tape one end to the head.

3 Cut out a construction paper forked tongue and tape it inside the snake's mouth. Cut out a construction paper pointed tail and tape it to the other end of the paper chain.

4 Tape a dowel to the tail and paint on eyes. Watch him slither! If you have only one dowel, use it for the tail and operate the head with your hand. (This snake also makes a great shadow puppet. See page 40.)

HOW TO FOLD YOUR ENVELOPE

2 Tortoise

Quick Starts Tips!™
How to Attach a Dowel

Place a dowel straight up and down on the back of your puppet. The dowel may go to the top of your puppet for support, but if it goes above, your audience will see it. At the bottom, leave plenty of room for your hand to operate the dowel. Tape in place. In the case of a large or a long puppet such as the Paper-Chain Wriggly Snake (see page 14), you may need to add two or three dowels.

3 Foil Fish

4 Bird

Stick Puppets

Stick puppets are a big favorite and for good reason:
they're easy to handle during a puppet show and
they lend themselves well to all types of characters.
Hunt for some old plastic gallon jugs, brooms, and
mops. These everyday items can be transformed
easily into cool cats, cute puppies,
and other neat characters.

MATERIALS

Blue craft foam, 1 sheet
Green, yellow, and orange craft
  foam, scraps
Pencil
Scissors
White glue
Wiggly eyes
1 dowel, about the thickness of a
  pencil, 12" {30 cm} long

Tropical fish can be found all over the world, in every size, shape, and color. This fish puppet will get you started, and then you can make a whole school of vibrantly colored fish. Look at pictures of real tropical fish or visit an aquarium to get inspired!

To MAKE THE SMILING FISH

1 There are templates for this puppet on page 55. Trace two fish shape onto the blue craft foam and cut them out. Label one side of each fish the front and one side the back.

2 Trace one stripe shape onto the green craft foam and one onto the yellow craft foam. Cut out and glue on as shown.

3 Trace four fin details and four tail details onto the orange craft foam and cut out. Glue on.

4 Glue a wiggly eye onto the front of each fish shape.

5 When the two sides are dry, apply a line of glue down the center of the back of one fish shape. Press the dowel onto the glue.

6 Apply glue to the back of the fish shape with the dowel on it and press the two shapes together with the dowel between them. Let dry.

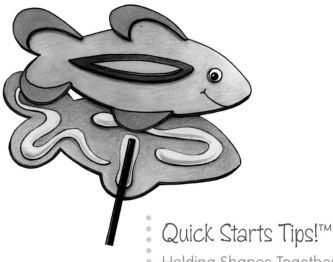

Quick Starts Tips!™
Holding Shapes Together
Use paper clips to hold the fish shapes together while they are drying.

Wish-Upon a Starfish

This simple stick puppet is sure to be a "star" in your show. Make a galaxy of starfish!

To MAKE THE WISH-UPON A STARFISH

1 There are templates for this puppet on page 56. Trace two starfish shapes onto the craft foam and cut them out. Use the red marker to draw spots on the front side of the starfish shapes.

2 Follow Steps 5 and 6 on page 17 to complete your starfish.

Beautiful Sea Jelly

This luminous, flowing sea jelly adds lots of color to your puppet show – make a few and let them show off in an undersea dance. With its flowing tentacles and easy operation, this sea jelly is fun to make, fun to use, and fun to watch!

To Make the Beautiful Sea Jelly

1 Cut an "X" 1/2" (1 cm) in diameter into the bottom of the plastic cup.

2 Cut out five strips of each color of tissue paper 1/2" x 18" (1 cm x 45 cm). The best way to do this is to leave the paper folded as it was in the package and cut through several layers at a time. Carefully separate the strips of tissue paper.

3 Take two strips of each color of tissue paper (10 strips total) and fasten them together at one end with tape. Tape the strips to the dowel about 1/2" (1 cm) from the top, leaving room for part of the dowel to poke through the cup.

4 Turn the cup upside down and push the dowel up through the "X" in the bottom of the cup.

5 Take three strips of each color of tissue paper (15 strips total) and gather in the center of the strips. Twist slightly.

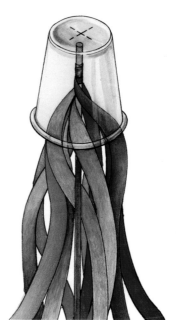

6 Apply glue to the part of the dowel sticking through the "X" in the cup and stick the twisted tissue paper strands to it so that they cascade over the outside of the cup. Use tape to secure the strands if necessary.

7 Glue wiggly eyes to the outside of the cup.

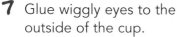

OTTO, the OCTOPUS

This friendly and colorful octopus makes a cute character for an underwater adventure.
Make the dangling tentacles sway to and fro as if he is swimming through the sea.

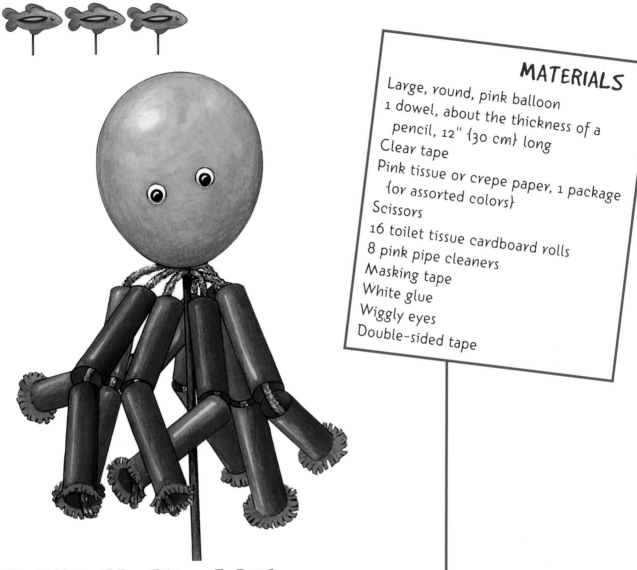

MATERIALS

Large, round, pink balloon
1 dowel, about the thickness of a pencil, 12" {30 cm} long
Clear tape
Pink tissue or crepe paper, 1 package {or assorted colors}
Scissors
16 toilet tissue cardboard rolls
8 pink pipe cleaners
Masking tape
White glue
Wiggly eyes
Double-sided tape

TO MAKE OTTO, THE OCTOPUS

1 Blow up the pink balloon so that it stands about 10" (25 cm) tall. Tape the balloon to the dowel above the knot.

2 Cover eight of the toilet tissue rolls with pieces of tissue paper, tucking it in at both ends. Use tape to secure the tissue paper on the outside.

3 Cover the remaining toilet tissue rolls with tissue paper, only this time, tuck the tissue paper into one end of the tube and cut the other end into tassels.

4 Bend each pipe cleaner at each end, about 1/2" (1 cm) down to form a hook at each end. Use masking tape to attach the pipe cleaners to the dowel right under the balloon.

5 Cut out a rectangle measuring 3" x 6" (7.5 cm x 15 cm) from three or four layers of tissue paper. Glue the layers together. Let dry. Glue to the top of the dowel, making a collar to cover the masking tape as shown (use tape to secure the collar if necessary). Cut fringe along the bottom.

6 Thread a pipe cleaner through each tube. Put the eight tubes without tassels closest to the balloon. Use the hook at the end of each pipe cleaner to hold the bottom tubes in place.

7 Use double-sided tape to attach the wiggly eyes to the balloon.

BEWARE OF BURSTING BALLOONS
To avoid bursting your balloons: Do not use a hot glue gun. Be careful of the sharp pipe cleaner ends. Don't try to remove tape from the balloon's surface. If your balloon pops, pick up all of the pieces. They are a choking hazard for young children.

Mops make great human, animal, and imaginative characters. Add large ears, eyes, noses, glasses, eyebrows, mustaches, hats, and neckties. You can even add arms cut out from poster board or cardboard to the mop handle.

Mr. Mophead

MATERIALS: 1 mop; craft foam, felt, or construction paper, scraps; scissors; tape, white glue, or a hot glue gun

Droopy-Eared Puppy

MATERIALS: 1 mop; 1 white bed sheet; 1 piece of string about 12" {30 cm} long; black and white craft foam, scraps; felt or construction paper, scraps; scissors; tape, white glue, or a hot glue gun

Très Cool Jughead Cat

The next time you finish a gallon of milk or water, wash the jug out and make a puppet! This cute kitty can be any kind you want it to be: black, white, tabby, or tiger. So drink up – you'll want enough gallon jugs to make a whole chorus of these cool cats!

MATERIALS

- 1 clear plastic gallon jug, well washed and rinsed, with lid
- 1/4-1/2 cup tempera paint, mixed with a little dish detergent, any color
- 4 black pipe cleaners
- Craft foam or construction paper, scraps
- Scissors
- White glue
- Broom handle or dowel

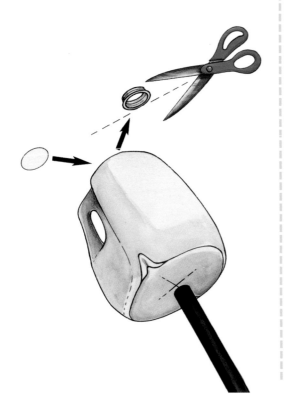

TO MAKE THE TRÈS COOL JUGHEAD CAT

1 Pour the tempera paint into the jug, replace the lid, and shake the jug until the inside surface is coated with paint. (Add a little water one teaspoon at a time if the paint isn't covering the inside.) Remove the lid and let dry.

2 Use the pipe cleaners to make whiskers. Cut out ears, a nose, and a tongue from the craft foam. Glue all pieces onto the jug.

3 Ask an adult to cut off the neck of the jug. Then, cut out an "X" on the bottom of the jug.

4 Cut out a circle with a diameter of 1 1/2" (4 cm) from the craft foam and glue it over the hole where the bottleneck was. Insert the broom handle into the "X."

Imagination Creations

When you're in a puppet mood, take a stroll through
your house — puppets will seem to appear out of the
blue! There's a lot you can create when you put your
mind to it. With a flashlight, an umbrella, or even a
feather duster, plus a good supply of craft materials,
you are well on your way to a fun
IMAGINATION CREATIONS
puppet show!

WHATCHAMACALLIT PUPPETS

After working your way through this chapter, you'll wonder, "Is there anything that can't be made into a puppet?" Feather dusters, umbrellas, flashlights, and even flower pots are just a few of the things that will spark your imagination and get you started!

 # Feather Duster Ostrich

As we were walking through the local dollar store, we saw the most colorful feather dusters. As soon as we saw them, we thought, "Ostrich!"

MATERIALS

1 feather duster
Wiggly eyes
White glue or hot glue gun
Feathers
Orange craft foam or
    construction paper, scraps
Scissors

To MAKE THE FEATHER DUSTER oSTRICH

1   Glue a wiggly eye to each side of the handle of the feather duster. If you have trouble attaching the eyes securely, ask an adult to help you use a hot glue gun for this step.

2   Glue feathers and an orange triangle beak cut out from the craft foam to the handle. To operate the puppet, just hide your hand under the feathers!

Umbrell-y Sea Jelly

While looking around the house for odds and ends, we spotted this umbrella tucked away in a coat closet. What to do with it? We worked together and came up with the idea for this marvelous puppet!

MATERIALS

Umbrella {use child-sized umbrellas for a school of smaller sea jellies}
2-3 rolls of crepe paper in different colors, or recycled gift wrap or tissue paper, cut into strips
Scissors
Tape
Black construction paper, scraps
1 Styrofoam ball, 2" {5 cm} diameter
Duct tape, Velcro tabs, or hot glue gun

To MAKE THE UMBRELL-Y SEA JELLY

1   Tape streamers to the inside edges of the umbrella. You can tape the strips randomly or in a pattern. Keep the strips very close together, slightly overlapping the edges.

2   Ask an adult to cut the Styrofoam ball in half. Cut out small circles from the construction paper for pupils and tape or glue them to the halves.

3   Fold and roll two pieces of duct tape (or use Velcro tabs) to attach the Styrofoam ball halves to the umbrella for eyes. Or, with an adult's help, use a hot glue gun to attach the eyes.

4   Open and close the umbrella very slowly to imitate the rhythmic motion of a floating sea jelly. This puppet looks great with a flashlight shining up into it.

Flash, the Flashlight Firefly

Did you know that fireflies aren't really flies at all? They're really beetles and are sometimes called lightning bugs. Turn off the lights, flash your flashlight beetle, and let it light up the stage for you!

MATERIALS

Small tube-shaped flashlight, about 9" {22.5 cm} long
Construction paper, 2 sheets of different colors
Pencil
Scissors
Colored markers
White glue
3 black pipe cleaners
Tissue paper, 1 sheet of any color
Double-sided tape

To MAKE FLASH, THE FLASHLIGHT FIREFLY

1 Trace around the bottom of the flashlight onto the construction paper. Cut out.

2 Draw a face or glue features cut from construction paper onto the circle. Glue the face to the bottom of the flashlight.

3 Wrap and twist one pipe cleaner around the end of the flashlight, close to the face. Curve the ends to look like antennae.

4 Form a number-8 shape from two pipe cleaners for wings. Glue the wings onto a piece of tissue paper. Trim around them when dry.

5 Use a piece of double-sided tape to attach the wings near the top of the flashlight.

Quick Starts Tips!™
Keeping Out of Sight
Wear a long-sleeved black shirt and a black glove to remain invisible while operating the puppet.

Bloomin' Flower Pot Puppet

These cute puppets are great for the outdoor scenes in your puppet show. Maybe you'd like some singing sunflowers or a chorus of chrysanthemums? These little puppets will add lots of laughter and color to your production (and they make great gifts, too).

MATERIALS

Old photo of yourself, a friend, or a family member (with permission)

Scissors

1 silk flower with a large circular center

White glue

1 flower pot with a drain hole at the bottom, or a peat pot, about 3" (7.5 cm) wide and 5" (12.5 cm) high

TO MAKE THE BLOOMIN' FLOWER POT PUPPET

1 Cut out a circle around the face in the photo so it fits the center of the flower. Glue the face onto the center of the flower.

2 Push the stem of the flower through the bottom of the flower pot. Bend the flower head a little so that the face points toward the audience.

3 The flower can grow in its pot if you push the stem upward, or disappear into its pot if you pull it down. Watch it steal the show!

Using one or two gloves and some craft supplies, these easy-to-create, easy-to-operate puppets are great for entertaining younger children.

The Happy Crab

Whoever heard of a happy crab? This critter is happy because it is snug and warm in a spare pair of gloves. It appears ready to walk smartly sideways down the beach.

MATERIALS

Red or orange knit gloves, 1 pair
White glue
Masking tape
1 red or orange pipe cleaner, cut in half
Wiggly eyes
Red or orange craft foam, 1 sheet
Pencil
Scissors

To MAKE THE HAPPY CRAB

1. Apply a thin line of glue along the outside thumb edges and down to the wrist of the gloves. Attach the gloves along the glue line. (Use some masking tape to hold them in place while they are drying.)

2 Thread half a pipe cleaner through each glove at the pointer finger knuckle. Form a T shape at the end of each, inside the glove, to prevent it from slipping out. Stick a small piece of masking tape over the T-shaped ends to prevent them from scratching you.

3 Form a small circle at the outside end of each pipe cleaner. Glue a wiggly eye on each circle.

4 There are templates for this puppet on page 57. Trace one shell and two claw shapes onto the craft foam and cut out.

5 Glue the claws to the thumbs of the gloves. Glue the shell to the top of the gloves as shown.

Quick Starts Tips!™
Attaching Gloves
For a quick and more secure way to attach the gloves in Step 1, ask an adult to help you use a hot glue gun or a needle and thread.

Handy, the Hedgehog

Hedgehogs are quite shy and roll into a ball with only their prickles showing when they are afraid. Introduce your hedgehog to your audience as a ball of prickles, then surprise them when its head pops out!

MATERIALS

Brown craft foam, 1 sheet
Brown fake fur
Ruler
Scissors
White glue
Paper clips
1 small black or brown pom pom, 1/8" {about 1/2 cm} diameter
Wiggly eyes
1 brown knit glove

TO MAKE HANDY, THE HEDGEHOG

1 Cut out a circle with a diameter of 6" (15 cm) from the brown craft foam, and a circle with a diameter of 4" (10 cm) from the fake fur.

2 Cut the craft foam circle in half. Form a cone with a base diameter of 2" (5 cm). Glue the cone edges together, using a paper clip to hold it in place while drying. This is the hedgehog's head.

3 Glue the pom pom onto the tip of the cone to make a nose. Glue on the wiggly eyes. Cut out two small ears from the craft foam and glue to the cone.

4 Glue the hedgehog's head to the underside of the glove on the pointer finger and middle finger.

5 Glue the fur circle from Step 1 on the top of the glove starting at the hedgehog's face. Use the glue in spots to allow it to stretch.

USE-IT-UP PUPPETS

It's time to dig into that craft box and recycle bin to see what leftover bits and pieces you can find to make these USE-IT-UP PUPPETS. Wiggly eyes, poster board, two-liter plastic bottles, paint, glue, glitter, and whatever else you can find — all have a purpose in the art of puppet-making!

Flying Butterfly

MATERIALS
1 pipe cleaner, any color
Floral wire {or wire that bends a little, but is strong enough to support a light object}, about 2" {5 cm} long
Needle-nose pliers
Tissue paper, 1 sheet
White glue
Scissors

These colorful butterflies can star in your puppet show or blend into the scenery for a realistic outdoor scene.

TO MAKE THE FLYING BUTTERFLY

1 Shape one pipe cleaner into butterfly wings. Attach the floral wire to the center of the butterfly wings. Use the needle-nose pliers to twist the wire tightly.

2 Glue a piece of tissue paper to each wing and decorate with tissue paper shapes cut out from scraps.

3 Once the glue has dried, trim the tissue paper around the wings.

Elephant with Swinging Trunk

This elephant puppet works well in a doorway theater with a curtain hung to hide your head and shoulders. Swing your arm (or trunk) side to side and pick up peanuts!

MATERIALS

Gray poster board or cardboard
    painted gray, about 22" x 28"
    {56 cm x 71 cm}
Pencil
Scissors
White poster board, 1 sheet
Black marker
White glue
Long gray sock

TO MAKE THE ELEPHANT WITH SWINGING TRUNK

1   There are templates for this puppet on page 58. Place the elephant head shape onto the gray poster board and trace the shape, but not the size, to draw a larger elephant head. Cut out.

2   Trace the tusk shape twice onto the white poster board and cut out. Cut out two circles from the white poster board for eyes. Color in the pupils with the black marker. Glue the tusks and eyes onto the elephant's head as shown.

3   Cut a circle under the elephant's eyes and above the tusks into which you can comfortably fit your arm (your arm will be the trunk). Start small — you can always make the hole bigger if necessary.

4   Put the sock on one arm and tuck the end between your thumb and fingers to look like the end of an elephant's trunk.

Storybook Puppet

This quick and easy puppet fits right on your hand and uses up extra felt or fabric scraps.

MATERIALS

Felt, 2 pieces about 8" x 12"
  {20 cm x 30 cm}, any color
Black marker or chalk
Scissors
White glue or needle and thread
Assorted craft supplies for decoration
Fabric scraps
Black marker

Fabric dress

TO MAKE THE STORYBOOK PUPPET

1 There is a template for this puppet on page 59. Place the two felt pieces on top of each other and trace around the body shape, including the head (use a black marker on light-colored felt or chalk on dark-colored felt), allowing a border of 1/2" (1 cm) all around. Cut out the two body shapes.

2 Glue around the edges of the felt, leaving an opening for your hand at the bottom. Press the two pieces together. Or, ask an adult to help you sew the two shapes together with a needle and thread.

3 Add yarn hair, bows, wiggly eyes, and a dress made out of printed fabric as shown. Draw on a mouth and nose.

More Quick Starts® Fun!

Make props to go along with your Storybook Puppet — perhaps a shepherd's staff made out of a pipe cleaner for a Heidi or Little Bo Peep character!

Lady Sings the Blues

Instead of throwing away those plastic two-liter soda bottles, make a wacky wide-mouthed puppet! These amusing characters are sure to be a hit at your puppet show.

MATERIALS

1 plastic bottle, 2-liter size, washed and rinsed
Scissors
Poster board or cardboard, 1 sheet
Black craft foam, 1 sheet
Pencil
Tape
Tempera paints, mixed with a little dish
    detergent, any skin tone color
Paintbrushes
Small lids or containers for paint
White glue
Pink craft foam, scraps
2 Styrofoam balls, 2" {5 cm} diameter
Yarn, 25 strands, about 2' {61 cm} long, any
    hair color
Fabric and lace or ribbon scraps

Quick Starts Tips!™
Making Puppets Taller
If you want your puppet to be taller, ask an adult to help you insert a broom handle into the neck of the bottle. Don't make it too tall — you'll still need to reach the head to operate the jaw.

To Make the Lady Sings the Blues

1 Ask an adult to help you cut out the bottle as shown. Trace twice around the cut bottle onto the poster board and twice onto the black craft foam. Cut out the circles.

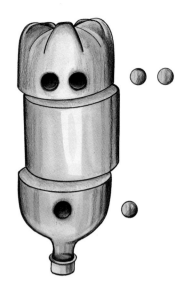

2 Tape the poster board circles to the open ends of the cut bottle.

3 Ask an adult to cut out holes in the back of the puppet's head for your pointer finger, middle finger, and thumb as shown.

4 Line up the holes you made for your fingers in the back and tape as shown. Allow the jaw to open and close easily.

5 Paint your puppet's face and let dry. When dry, glue the two black craft foam circles from Step 1 on top of the other circles inside the puppet's mouth. Cut out a tongue shape from the pink craft foam and glue it onto the lower black circle.

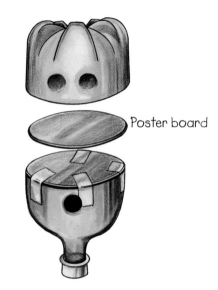

Poster board

6 Ask an adult to cut the Styrofoam balls in half. Paint one half the same color as your puppet head for the nose. Paint a black pupil on two halves for eyes. Let dry before gluing the nose and eyes to the puppet's face.

7 Cut strands of yarn to make hair. Tie the strands together in the middle. Glue or tape the hair to the top of the puppet's head. (To make bangs, cut shorter strands and glue or tape them to the top of the head in front of the longer strands.)

8 Tie fabric around the neck of the bottle to hide your hand. Glue a strip of lace or ribbon to any frayed fabric edges.

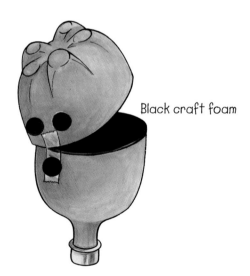

Black craft foam

9 To operate the puppet, hold the neck beneath the fabric with one hand and operate the jaw with the other.

Yarn hair

PAINTED-HAND PUPPETS

Transform your hands into fun characters for a puppet show. Please remember to put a layer of newspaper down on the table or floor before you begin working with paint.

The Better-to-Eat-You Alligator

Cut out two rows of teeth from white poster board. Paint one hand green. Paint an eye on the side of your hand just below your pointer finger knuckle, and a nostril at the end of your pointer finger. While the paint is still wet and sticky, stick one row of teeth on your thumb. Hold the other row of teeth between your pointer finger and middle finger.

Bonita, the Box Turtle

Paint your hand any color and paint an eye on the side of your pointer finger. When dry, tuck your fingers inside and move your puppet slowly. To make a shell, balance or tape a scooped-out baked potato skin on the back of your hand.

Robbie, the Rooster

There are templates for this puppet on page 61. Trace one rooster's comb onto red craft foam and two beaks onto orange craft foam. Cut out. Cut out circles for eyes from black and white construction paper. Paint one hand brown and, while the paint is still wet and sticky, attach the eyes. Ask a friend to use an elastic band to attach the beak to your thumb and pointer finger. Wrap the tail of the comb around your middle finger and glue or tape it in place.

Bird-in-Hand

Paint your hands with any design. Stick a small wiggly eye to each thumb as shown and wrap your thumbs around each other. Hold a small beak cut out from orange craft foam between your thumbs.

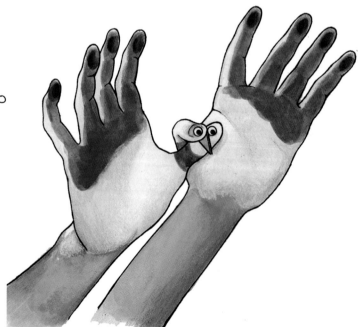

Happy Fisherman

There are templates for this puppet on page 62. Trace one hat and one fish shape onto yellow craft foam and cut out. Make a fishing pole with 6" (15 cm) of fishing wire and a toothpick. Use tape to attach the fish to the end of the wire. Paint one hand yellow, except for the tip of your pointer finger, middle finger, and thumb. Wrap the tail of the hat around your pointer finger and use glue or tape to hold it in place. Have the fisherman puppet hold the fishing pole with your thumb and middle finger.

Rainbow-Colored Butterfly

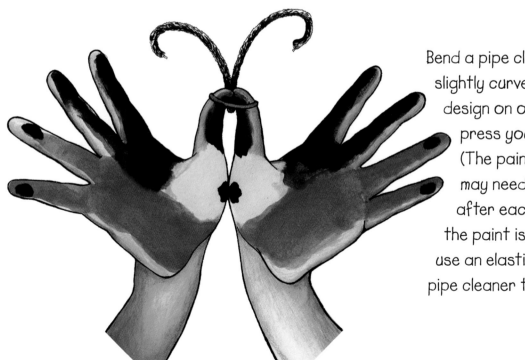

Bend a pipe cleaner in half and slightly curve each end. Paint your design on one palm, and then press your palms together. (The paint dries quickly, so you may need to press together after each color is added.) When the paint is dry, ask a friend to use an elastic band to attach the pipe cleaner to your thumbs.

Super Shadow Puppets & Shadow Theaters

One of the best things about shadow puppets is that you don't have to be an artist to make them! Find pictures in old magazines, use old photos, or print pictures from your computer. Trace the shapes onto poster board, cut them out, attach a dowel, and voila! you have a shadow puppet! Think up fun themes for your plays — a farmer and his animals, sports, the solar system, and underwater creatures all make good shows.

SUPER SHADOW PUPPETS
Once you make these shadow puppets, you'll see how they work. Then, use your imagination and improvise. You'll soon see that the sky's the limit!

Boy with Dog

Think about other shadow puppets you could attach with string. How about a monkey hanging from a tree by its tail made of string, or a child on a swing? Or perhaps a ship being towed by a tugboat? Keep the string or yarn thick enough so that it shows up in the shadows.

MATERIALS

Poster board or card stock, 1 sheet
Pencil
Scissors
White glue
Tape
2 dowels, each about the thickness of a pencil, 12" {30 cm} long
Thick yarn or string, 3-4" {7-10 cm} long

TO MAKE THE BOY WITH DOG

1 There are templates for this puppet on page 61. Trace one boy and one dog shape onto the poster board and cut out.

2 Tape or glue one dowel to the back of the dog and one to the back of the boy. (See HOW TO ATTACH A DOWEL, page 15.)

3 Tape a short length of yarn or string from the boy's hand to the dog's collar for a leash.

Grab-Some-Air Skateboarder

MATERIALS

Poster board or card stock, 1 sheet
Pencil
Scissors
Hole punch
1 brass paper fastener
2 dowels, each about the thickness
   of a pencil, 12" {30 cm} long
Tape or white glue

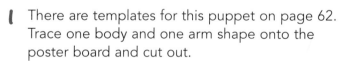

Move the puppet's arm and body just as skateboarders in action do.

To MAKE THE GRAB-SOME-AIR SKATEBOARDER

1 There are templates for this puppet on page 62. Trace one body and one arm shape onto the poster board and cut out.

2 Punch out a hole in the shoulder area of the arm and the shoulder area of the body. Use a brass paper fastener to attach the arm to the body.

3 Tape or glue one dowel to the back of the skateboarder's body and one to the back of his arm.

Slinky Double Dragon

MATERIALS

Poster board or card stock, 1 sheet
Pencil
Scissors
Hole punch
White copy paper, 1 sheet
Ruler
Tape
2 dowels, each about the thickness
   of a pencil, 12" {30 cm} long
White glue
Orange or red tissue paper, scraps

TO MAKE THE SLINKY DOUBLE DRAGON

1 There are templates for this puppet on page 60.
   Trace one head, one tail, and two foot shapes onto
   the poster board and cut out. Punch out an eye
   hole in the head.

2 Cut out a rectangle 8" x 1 ½" (20 cm x 4 cm)
   from the white copy paper and fan-fold it to
   make the body.

3 Fold the head and tail as shown on the templates.
   Tape the head to one end of the body, the tail to
   the other end, and one foot to each end. Tape or
   glue one dowel to the head and one to the tail.

4 Cut out thin strips about 2" (5 cm) long from the
   tissue paper and tape them to the mouth of the
   dragon to look like flames.

HOW TO FAN-FOLD

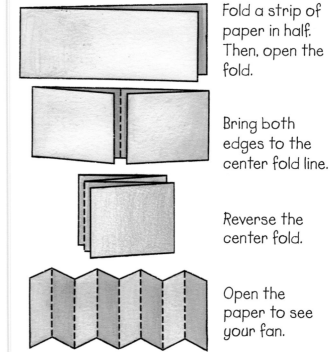

Fold a strip of
paper in half.
Then, open the
fold.

Bring both
edges to the
center fold line.

Reverse the
center fold.

Open the
paper to see
your fan.

1-2-3 SHADOW PUPPET THEATERS

The most important thing about shadow puppets is, well, their shadows! You will want to keep two things in mind when creating your shadow puppet theater: the size of your screen and lighting the screen.

Take a minute to think about your audience. The farther away from your viewers you'll be, the bigger your screen should be. Experiment with large and small screens (using a white sheet, white paper, or waxed paper) depending on the size of your puppets. Now, think about lighting. To make the puppet silhouettes really stand out, place a lamp without its shade or a desk lamp on a table or pedestal behind you — leave enough room between the light source and the screen for you to control your puppets. For the best results, put on your shadow plays in a darkened room.

LIGHT SAFETY
Please be sure to place the lamp where it won't tip over and it won't touch any curtains, paper, or person. The uncovered bulb can become very hot.

QUICK STARTS TIPS!™ FOR SHADOW PUPPETS

Your shadow puppets will look clearer if you have a smooth screen. To avoid wrinkles, gently stretch the fabric or paper and then attach it.

The outline of your shadow puppet is the most important part, so trace carefully. When cutting out your shape, don't forget the smaller areas, such as the spaces between arms and bodies.

If the light shines through your poster board shapes, make your shape two layers thick with the dowel between them.

Practice making shadows with your hands instead of using puppets. You can add an alligator head made from cardboard to your hand, or a head to the end of one finger and use your other fingers as arms.

Use an old piece of Styrofoam as a stand for your puppets when you're not using them. Just poke the ends of the dowels into it.

If you do not have dowels to use for your shadow puppets, you may also use unsharpened pencils. Or, use wire from an old coat hanger (ask an adult to cut it for you) or craft wire.

On with the Show!

So, your puppets are all dressed up with nowhere to go? It's time to put on your director's cap and plan your show! There's a lot to do: you'll need to think about who will be in your audience, build the theater, write the puppet script, draw or paint the scenery, decide what props to use, and of course, practice using your puppets. Once everything is in place, it's time for lights, camera, action!

1-2-3 EASY PUPPET THEATERS

The simplest puppet theater is no theater at all! That's right, just hold the puppets high in front of you and say your lines "in character."

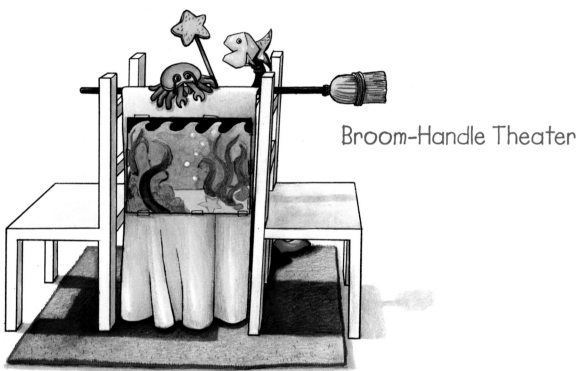

Broom-Handle Theater

For many puppets, the puppeteers only need to crouch down behind the back of a sofa. Or, hang a curtain on a spring-loaded curtain rod in a doorway for another great "instant" theater. For outdoor fun, tie a rope between two trees and hang a sheet over the rope. Now crouch down behind the sheet and let the show begin.

Doorway Theater

Cardboard Box Theater

Quick Starts Tips!™

Choosing a Box

Cardboard boxes of any size can be transformed into puppet theaters. Visit a household appliance store to look for large discarded boxes — some are so big that you can step right into them! If you have trouble fitting the box into the car, open the ends and fold it flat, then just rebuild it with strong tape when you're ready to build your theater.

Look for cardboard boxes at your grocery store, too. Remember, boxes can be cut and used for props, background, and scenery.

MATERIALS

Cardboard box, any size
X-Acto knife {adult use only}
Tempera paints, any colors
Paintbrushes
Small lids or containers for paint
Assorted craft supplies for decoration
White glue or tape

TO MAKE THE CARDBOARD BOX THEATER

1 Depending on the size of your box, stand it up vertically or lay it down horizontally on a tabletop. Ask an adult to cut an opening for the screen.

2 Decorate your theater. Glue or tape fabric curtains to the inside of the box, and posters of show times and pictures of characters from your show to the outside of the box. If you like, add a poster board frame around the screen.

More Quick Starts® Fun!

For a fancier backdrop in your theater, poke a hole on either side near the back of the cardboard box and insert a dowel with a small fabric curtain. Use fabric with stars on it for an outer space show or with jungle animals on it for a rain forest scene.

PUPPET OPERATION

To operate a puppet, you need your fingers, wrists, arms, elbows, and shoulders.

It can get tiring holding up a puppet for a long time, so you may want to prop one arm up with the other. Hold your arm at a right angle to the floor to prevent your puppet from leaning to the side or resting on the stage — otherwise your audience may think your puppet (or its puppeteer) is sleeping! Keep your puppets awake! Make sure they are active and fun to watch, not just standing around.

If the stage is higher than your audience, tilt the puppet down a little. Remember to keep the puppet high enough for the audience to see it.

When a puppet is speaking, it should be the center of attention and facing the audience. If two or more puppets are talking to each other, they should be facing each other. As the words of the play are being spoken, the puppet's mouth should be opening and closing — move the lower jaw slightly for the most realistic look. When the puppet is shocked, surprised, or screaming, open its mouth wide!

Match each puppet's personality with the voices of your puppeteers. For example, a happy tone fits the personality of the Smiling Fish (page 17) and a deeper voice works well for The Better-to-Eat-You Alligator (page 37).

Think of interesting ways for your puppet to enter the stage. Maybe a big leap to shock or frighten the audience, or a slow, magical elevation. Or, make your puppet appear to be walking up a staircase to the stage — when it leaves, make sure it goes back down the staircase!

Practice your puppet show in front of a mirror or videotape your rehearsals to see where improvements can be made. Try to perfect the timing of sounds with actions on stage.

Make sure to have enough hands for the puppets that will appear on stage at the same time. Be sure the crew who are in charge of the lights, sound, scene changes, and special effects wear dark clothes so they are less likely to be noticed.

Finally, get organized backstage! Arrange your puppets in the order of their appearance.

SCRIPTING THE SHOW

Every good puppet show, like every good story, needs a beginning, a middle, and an end. Whether you are writing your own script or adapting one of your favorite stories into a puppet show, it's important to remember these three important ingredients. Think of it as a three-act play.

Look for puppet show scripts at your local library, at theater supply stores, or, with an adult's permission, on the internet. When writing your script, include directions for the puppeteers. A good puppet show script notes when and where each puppet should appear on stage. Make a copy of the script for each puppeteer (and the people working the props, lighting, sound, and scene changes), with each puppeteer's role highlighted. Each puppeteer can follow along, listening for cues to enter the stage, to speak, to dance, or whatever his action may be. This will help your show go off without a hitch!

To keep the show moving, consider using a narrator. The narrator will help move the show along by giving background about the story and speaking to the audience during scene changes.

A NOTE ABOUT PUPPETEERS

The puppeteers in your show are just as important as the puppets themselves! They should be dressed in black shirts and dark pants. When they are speaking, they should speak very loudly – as if they are trying to throw their voice – and when they're not speaking, they should keep quiet and out of sight.

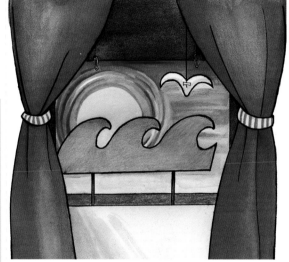

SETTING THE SCENE

Different scenery can be painted onto large sheets of paper or poster board and switched at scene changes during the show. Hang the scenery on fishing wire with paper clips, pin or tape it to a fabric background, or use Velcro tabs to attach it. Once you have your background, get creative with the set design!

DEFINE THE PLACE

Think about where your puppets might live or where you would like them to perform. Do they live underwater? In outer space? Are they at the playground? Here are some ideas for set design to get you started:

• For an underwater scene, glue or tape outlines of waves to the bottom of your screen. Or, attach sticks to wave shapes and move them up and down. You could even blow bubbles in front of the light source for a cool effect.

• For an outer space scene, glue or tape planets to your screen, or let them hang from an overhead dowel.

• If your puppets are outside, use real branches to look like trees. Place them close to the screen and anchor them to pieces of cardboard with modeling clay. For falling autumn leaves, cut leaf shapes from construction paper and drop them in front of the light source. For snow or rain, sprinkle confetti made from white or blue construction paper between the light and the screen.

QUICK CHANGE!

Here's a simple trick to show changes in the time of day or season. Cut out from poster board or craft foam the shape of a sun and the shape of a moon. Stick the sun shape to one side of a wooden spoon and the moon shape to the other. Using the same idea, you can make a tree with green leaves on one side and fall-colored leaves on the other. Or, make faces — happy on one side, sad on the other, or awake on one side, asleep on the other.

LIGHT IT UP!

Lighting is especially important in a puppet show — you'll want the audience to see the stars of the show, of course! There's a lot you can do with a couple of desk lamps and flashlights, so start experimenting!

• Position the light higher or lower than your hands to avoid casting unwanted shadows.

• Turn off the room lights during your show, just as they do in a theater.

• Adjustable lighting is good for changing scenes from day to night. Use a bright table lamp for daytime and a dim flashlight for evening.

• A flashlight makes a great movable spotlight to bring attention to one particular character during your show — it's his big scene, after all!

• To light up a large screen, use two or three desk lamps or some clamp-on reading lights. Use a flashlight for a small screen.

• When changing scenes during your performance, turn off the puppet theater lights and turn on the room lights. This way, you can change the set without your audience seeing.

• If you are experimenting alone with lighting, set up a mirror in front of your screen to see how the lighting is working. Or, ask a friend to help.

SOUND & SPECIAL EFFECTS

Get creative with sound and special effects. These special touches keep your puppet show lively, interesting, and entertaining! Here are some ideas to inspire you:

SUPER SOUND EFFECTS

• Use cymbals or two pan lids to create a great crashing sound for a thunderstorm effect. (Hold poster board at the ends and shake it for another great thunder sound.)

• Bang two plastic cups together to sound like a horse's hooves.

• Drop a container of pennies or metal bottle caps for a loud crash.

• Use musical instruments to create sound effects for your puppet show.

• Use a hairdryer or a handheld vacuum cleaner to make the sound of a plane or car engine.

• Close a book quickly for the sound of a slamming door.

• Blow bubbles through a straw into a cup of water for a bubbling sound.

• Roll small rocks or dried beans around in a pan for the sound of rain.

• Play appropriate music during the scene changes and before and after the show to set the mood and keep your audience's attention. Or, play and sing along to songs during your performance!

• Before your performance, tape the sounds that you need in the order you need them. Then, just play the tape during the show.

SUPER SPECIAL EFFECTS

• Blow bubbles for a realistic underwater scene.

• Use silver tinsel attached to a dowel or a strip of sturdy cardboard for rain. You can also hang the tinsel from fishing line or attach it to sticks on either end of the top of the theater.

• A flashlight or a camera flash makes a great lightning effect.

• Make a whale puppet spray water by using a squirt gun hidden behind it.

• Run a humidifier for a foggy scene.

• Use colored light bulbs: blue for underwater scenes, red for a sunset.

Puppet Templates

For several of the puppets in this book, you are asked to trace a template. You'll need tracing paper, a pencil, scissors, cereal-box cardboard, and an envelope or zipper-styled sandwich bag.

To MAKE PUPPET TEMPLATES

1 Trace the template onto tracing paper and cut out. Then, trace it onto the cardboard, label it just as it is labeled in the book, and cut out.

2 Follow the rest of the instructions for the puppet you are making.

3 Then, put all of the templates for a particular puppet in an envelope or a zipper-styled sandwich bag. Label with the name of the project, such as "Smiling Fish." That way, you can reuse your templates many times and share them with your friends.

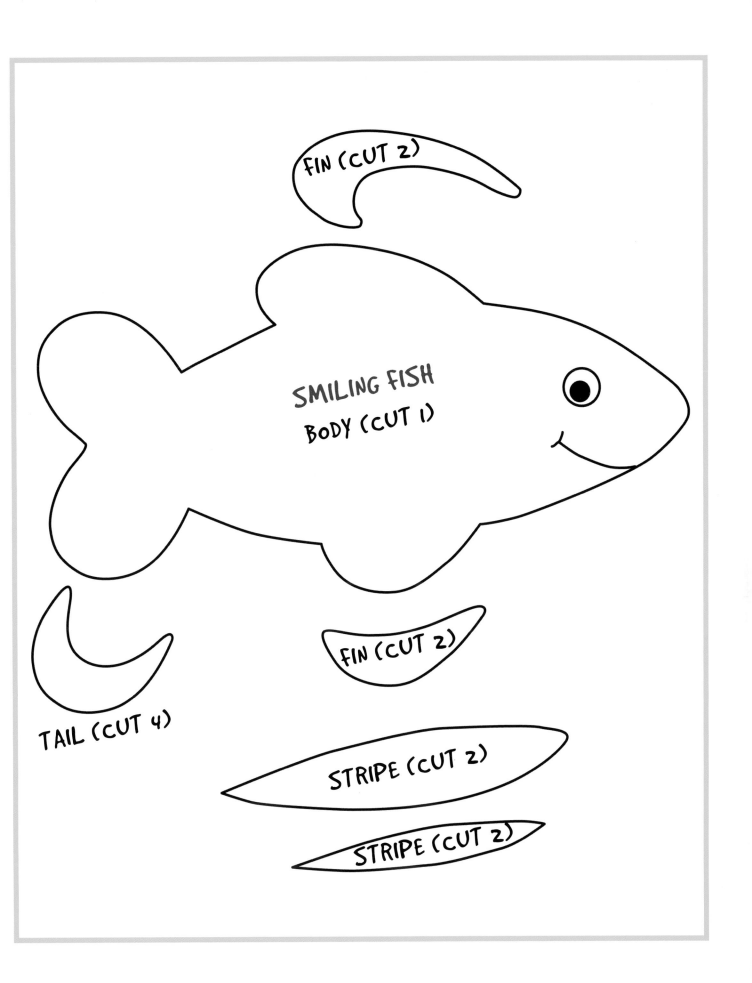

WISH-UP ON A STARFISH
STARFISH (CUT 2)

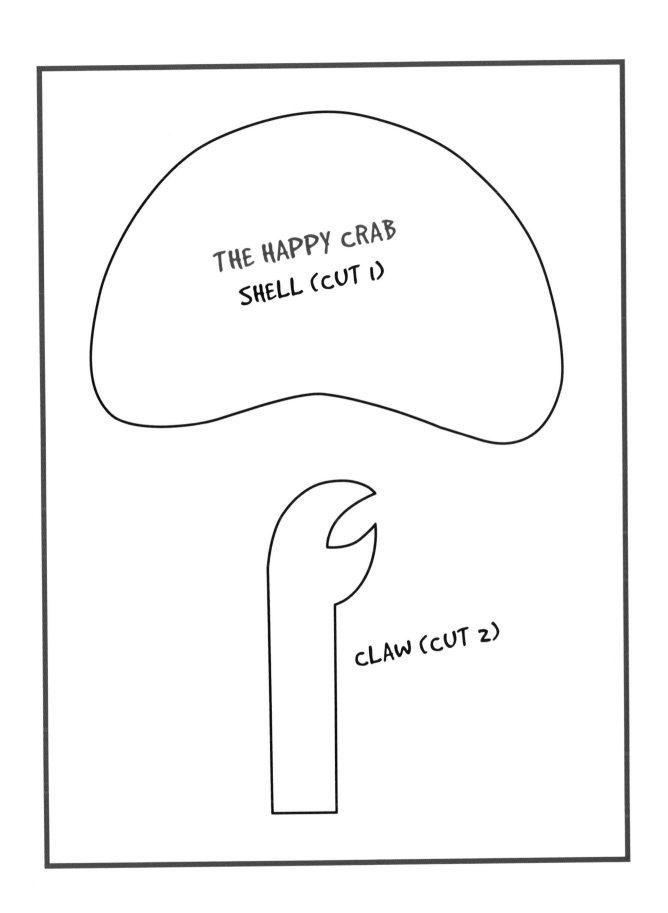

THE HAPPY CRAB
SHELL (CUT 1)

CLAW (CUT 2)

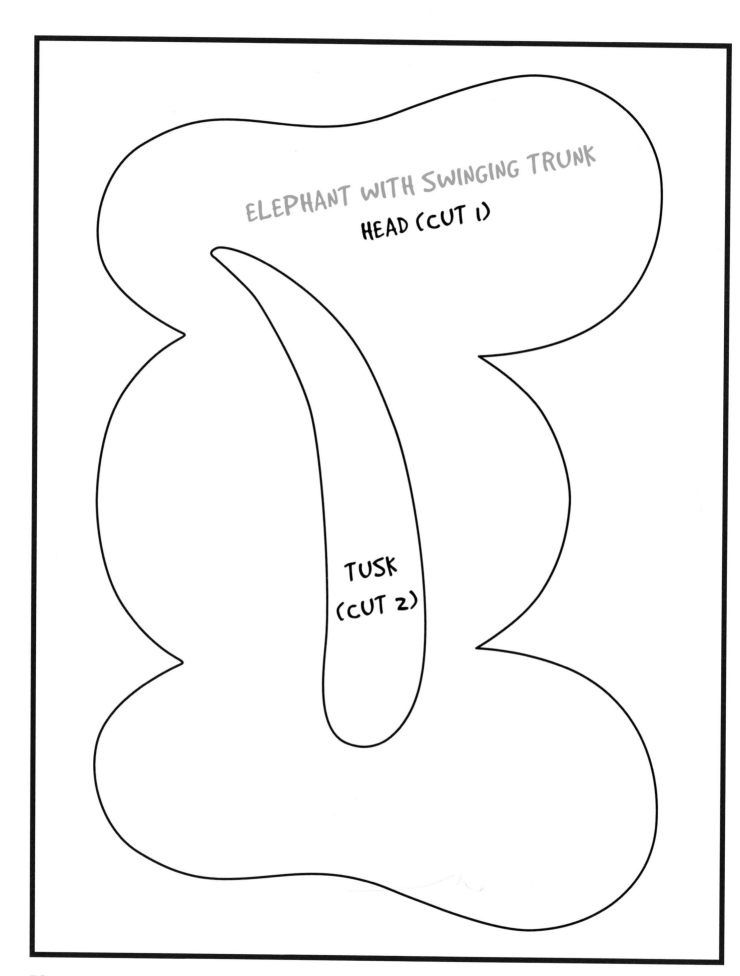

ELEPHANT WITH SWINGING TRUNK

HEAD (CUT 1)

TUSK
(CUT 2)

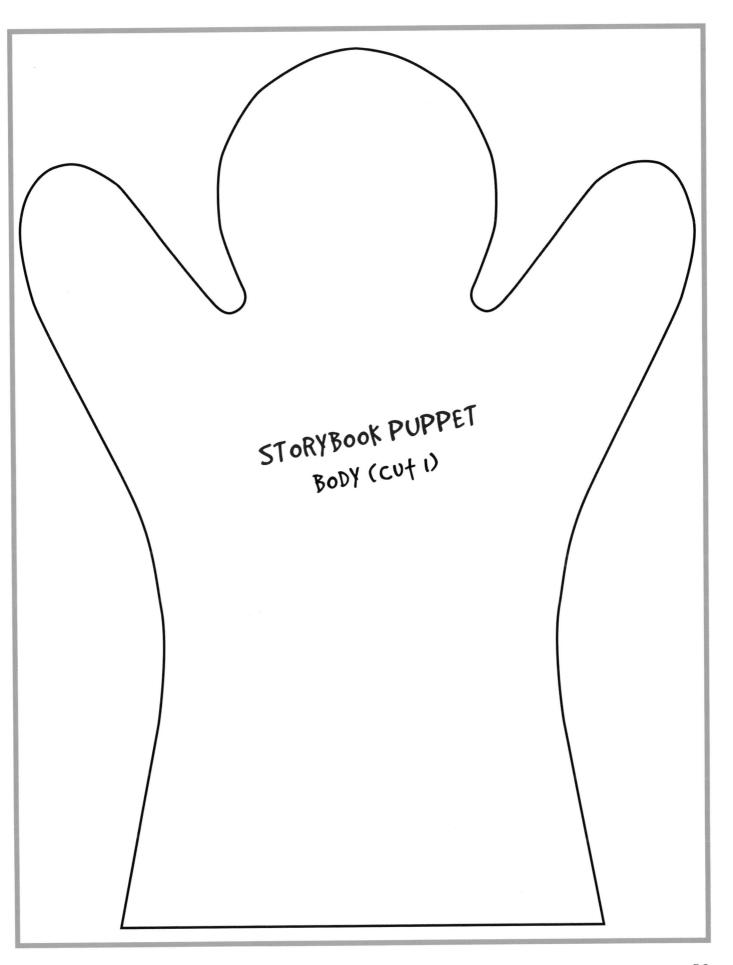

STORYBOOK PUPPET
BODY (CUT 1)

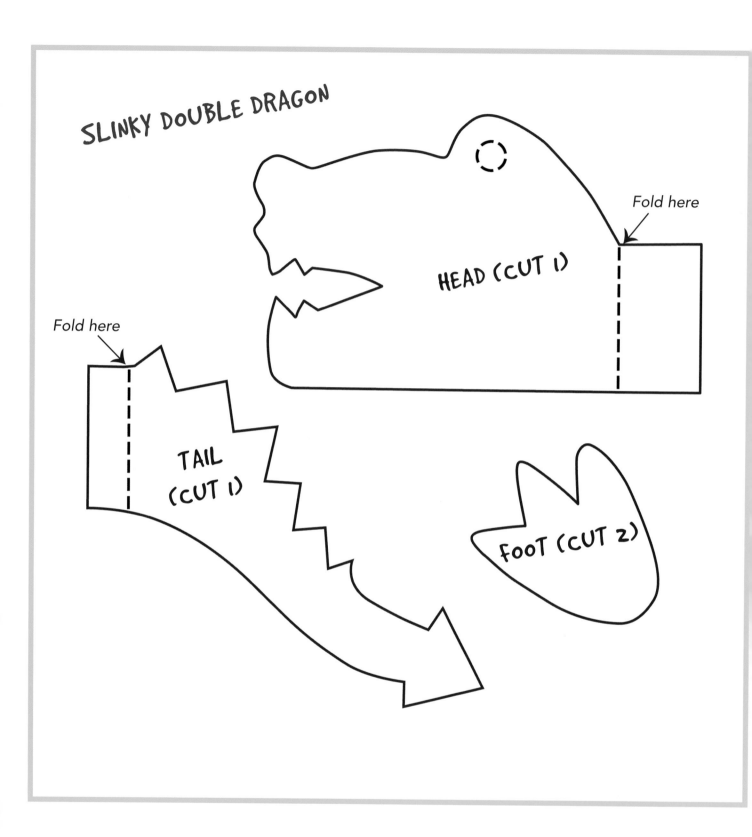

SLINKY DOUBLE DRAGON

Fold here

HEAD (CUT 1)

Fold here

TAIL (CUT 1)

FOOT (CUT 2)

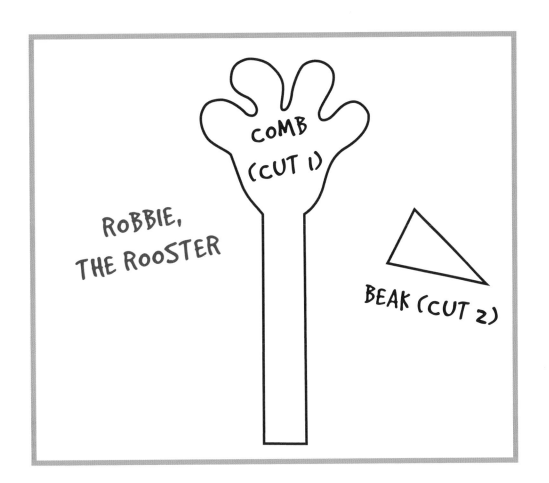

GRAB-SoME-AIR
SKATEBOARDER

ARM (CUT 1)

BODY (CUT 1)

HAT
(CUT 1)

HAPPY FISHERMAN

FISH
(CUT 1)

Index

Quick Starts Tips!™ & Techniques

Puppet Templates

More *Quick Starts for Kids!*® from Williamson Books!

 If you like to craft, create, and keep busy with fun things to do, you may be interested in our other books. All *Quick Starts for Kids!*® books are for people of all ages from 8 to 88! 64 pages, fully illustrated, trade paper, 8 ½ x 11, $8.95 US (higher in Canada). To order, please see below.

KIDS' EASY KNITTING PROJECTS

In full color!
KNITTING II
More Easy-to-Make Knitting Projects

Parents' Choice Approved
BAKE THE BEST-EVER COOKIES!

KIDS' EASY BIKE CARE
Tune-Ups, Tools & Quick Fixes

40 KNOTS TO KNOW
Hitches, Loops, Bends & Bindings

Dr. Toy 100 Best Children's Products
Dr. Toy 10 Best Socially Responsible Products
MAKE YOUR OWN BIRDHOUSES & FEEDERS

CREATE YOUR OWN CANDLES
30 Easy-to-Make Designs

GARDEN FUN!
Indoors & Out; In Pots & Small Spots

MAKE YOUR OWN COOL CARDS
25 Awesome Notes & Invitations!

ForeWord Magazine Book of the Year Finalist
DRAWING HORSES
(that look *real!*)

Oppenheim Toy Portfolio Gold Award
DRAW YOUR OWN CARTOONS!

Parents' Choice Recommended
ALMOST-INSTANT SCRAPBOOKS

MAKE YOUR OWN HAIRWEAR
Beaded Barrettes, Clips, Dangles & Headbands

REALLY COOL FELT CRAFTS

KIDS' EASY QUILTING PROJECTS

YO-YO!
Tips & Tricks from a Pro

BE A CLOWN
Techniques from a Real Clown

MAKE YOUR OWN FUN FRAMES